Put on a Happy Face

Mama Clown's Complete
How-to Book of Face Painting

by

Marcela Murad
"Mama Clown"

Venture Press
Fort Lauderdale, FL

Photography by Alan Wilco

Dedicated with love and thanks to the happy faces
in this book: Stephanie, Vickie, Jayson, Sara,
Heather, Lisa, Jessie, Melisa, Brent, Bryan, Shanti,
Samantha, Maggie, Dustin, Jorel and Cade. Special
thanks to my Dad, Jimmy Pizarro, and to my sister,
Claudia Banks, who made this dream a reality.
I love you all.

CONTENTS

FACE PAINTING BASICS

Welcome to the wonderful world of face painting. My name is Marcela Murad. I live and work in Hollywood, Florida, as a professional clown known as "Mama Clown." I perform magic, work with balloons, even juggle a little, but face painting is my favorite pastime.

Most kids love to have their faces painted so that they can pretend to be ferocious tigers, enchanting fairy princesses, superheroes, or scary monsters. Parents can paint the faces of their own children, and children can even share in the fun by painting each other, using the designs described in this book.

Face painting is an art, and like all art forms has no limits. What can be created is limited only by the face painter's imagination. Although I've subtitled this book *The Complete Guide to Face Painting*, it is impossible to include all of the

possible styles and combinations of designs in a single book. In fact, the number of designs that are possible is infinite. However, this book is complete in that it accurately describes the steps for applying face painting makeup and provides a large variety of examples to learn from. With the techniques I provide in this book you will be able to create an unlimited number of original designs of your own.

The feelings I get from watching faces being transformed into the designs described within these pages is something I wish everyone who picks up this book will choose to experience. The sparkle in children's eyes and the expression of their personalities as they see themselves in the mirror fills me with the warmth and innocence of my own childhood. Their joy helps me to remember, as I grow up (or old), that age is nothing but

a state of mind, and the kingdom of heaven is found in a child-like heart.

Is face painting just for small children? Not at all. Although young children generally get the most excitement out of having their faces painted, teenagers and adults also enjoy wearing many of the face designs and tattoos described in this book. Most younger children prefer the animals, funny faces, and superheroes while teenagers and adults prefer the fantasy and scary faces. Tattoos appeal equally to all age groups.

The designs in this book were created over a nine year period—some purely out of my own imagination, like the Rainbowland Princess. Others were inspired by the beautiful work of a dear friend and fellow face painter, Michelle Newman. (Thanks Michelle, bet you didn't know you were my inspiration!) Still, most of them, such as the animals and superheroes, came from studying pictures in books and magazines.

Most of the designs, though they may appear difficult at first glance, are relatively easy to do. If you are artistically inclined, you won't have any problem developing you own style and using you own creativity. If you aren't, don't worry...anyone can learn to face paint. All of the designs have been simplified and structured to consume as little time as possible, even for beginners. By studying the pictures and following the simple instructions, you will be able to face paint the first time you go through the book. The more you enjoy doing it, the faster you'll become a pro. With this in mind, allow me to introduce and explore the wonderful art of face painting with you.

May you experience the happy faces of many little ones in the years to come.

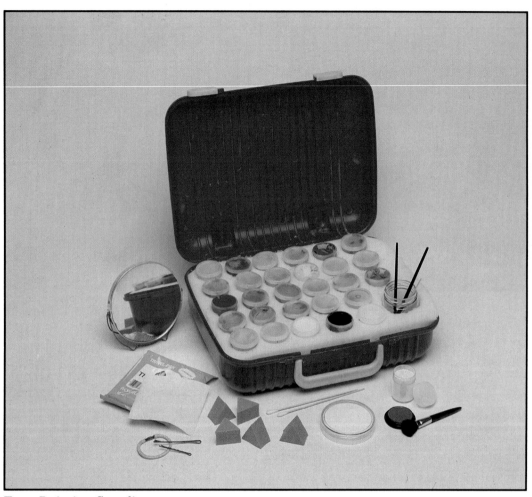

Face Painting Supplies

MATERIALS

Materials you will need for face painting are:
- Water-soluble cosmetic paints
- Brushes
- Cosmetic sponges
- Container of water
- Baby wipes
- Mirror
- Headband and/or hair clips
- Towel (small terry cloth)
- Powder blush and brush
- Eyeshadow (optional)
- Glitter (optional)
- Mascara (optional)
- Color hair spray (optional)
- Fake blood (optional)
- Case to carry your materials

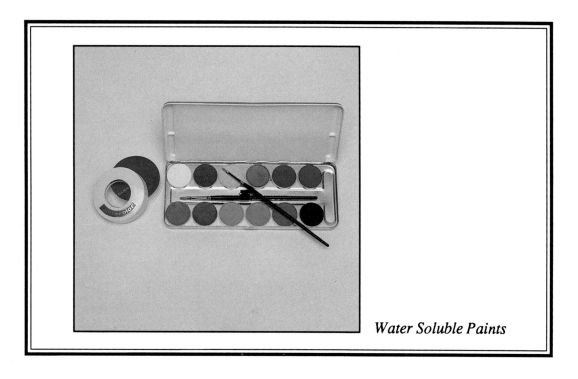

Water Soluble Paints

Paints

When I first started face painting, I used the same oil-based greasepaint that professional makeup artists wear and that I wear on my own clown face. What a mess!!! This type of makeup smears and comes off easily on hands, clothes, or whatever it comes in contact with because it always remains moist unless covered with a makeup powder. Also, being oil-based, it will not wash off easily with just ordinary soap and water. When I used this type of paint it would smear and get all over everything. Most of the greasepaint wouldn't come off clothes or furniture. Now that I think about it, I'm lucky people didn't get very angry with me.

For a little while I tried finger paints, but they were too runny. Then I discovered water-soluble makeup. Unlike the finger paints, water-soluble makeup is made for the skin and produces much better quality colors. This makeup is easy to apply and washes off with just soap and water. It also washes out of clothes and furniture. It is non-toxic and completely safe for use on the face. After being applied, it dries quickly and won't smear.

For children, water-soluble makeup is clearly preferable to theatrical greasepaint. Look for makeup marked "non-toxic" and "safe for skin and hair".

The only problem I've encountered with water-soluble makeup is that it will come off just as easily with a messy ice cream cone or drippy soda as it will with water. Although the paint is non-toxic, eating messy foods can smear the design.

Many companies manufacture water-soluble makeup. I've experimented with most of the different types and brands of water-soluble cosmetic paints, looking for colors that were bright, did not fade rapidly, dried fast, and would not smear easily. After testing the majority of them, I ended up combining the different brands to produce a top quality kit for my own personal use. Although there are many good quality brands of makeup available, the brands of my choice are Kryolan and Mehron. Kryolan has excellent texture and the widest selection of colors. I use Mehron Starbright White to cover the entire face; I also like their brushes.

Theatrical and cosmetic makeup is typically referred to as foundation. Much of the makeup you see will be labeled with this term. Water-soluble makeups are frequently called pancake foundation. When shopping for makeup for face painting, look for the terms pancake or water-soluble on the label.

Although some cosmetics contain red dyes that can irritate the skin around the eyes or cause an allergic reaction, most dyes in good quality water-soluble cosmetics are safe and have been approved for use around the eyes. Do not use any kind of paint that is not made specifically for face painting. Some of the chemicals in such paints are made to be used on other surfaces—not on the delicate skin of a child—and can cause irritation or an allergic reaction. Be cautious; you want to "put on a happy face", not a sad or an angry one. It's better to be safe than sorry.

If you are a beginner, start with a palette containing six basic colors: black, white, blue, green, yellow, and red. As you gain experience, you will want to add fancy colors such as turquoise, hot pink, purple, and the metallics. Having these colors will stimulate your imagination and can also be used to match a child's hair, eye color, and clothing, thus creating an even more professional look.

Basic face painting and makeup supplies are available at most good novelty, toy and drug stores. You can also find an excellent selection of paints and makeups at theatrical or dance supply stores. See the appendix for a list of makeup suppliers.

Brushes

There are many types of brushes, ranging in quality from theatrical sable hair brushes sold by quality makeup suppliers to simple craft and hobby brushes obtainable at toy and hobby stores.

Brushes come in various sizes and are usually marked with a number designating the relative width. For example, a #1 brush is used for very thin lines like mustache or eyebrow hairs; a #2 or #4 brush for thicker lines such as outlining around the clown's mouth; and a wide #10 brush for very thick lines like zebra stripes.

I like to use a #6 white nylon brush—one that ends in a square rather than a point—which enables me to draw thin straight lines. Brush manufacturers use various numbering systems so that a #2 from one company may not be exactly the same as the #2 from another. Most of the time you will have to choose visually the brush sizes you want.

Inexpensive craft and hobby paint brushes as well as cotton swabs such as Q-tips can be used to apply makeup. However, I feel that a good brush is your most important tool and the one that has the most influence on your results. Through much experimenting, I have found the best and most durable brush to be a Mehron stageline theatrical makeup brush with a square tip made out of nylon. I use three sizes: the #314 for most work, the smaller #312 for fine detail and the broad #316 to color large areas, as in the Batman design. I keep a supply on hand, but use no more than three at a time. I use a single brush for all colors. When changing colors I rinse the brush off with water and wipe it off on a napkin or baby wipe.

Sponges

Sponges are used when you need to apply a large amount of paint to the face. Some faces, like the clown's faces, require a coat of white paint over the entire face. A sponge can hold more paint and can spread the paint more evenly over larger areas than a brush, thus producing better results. Use regular cosmetic sponges available at your local drugstore or makeup supplier. As with the brushes, keep a good supply on hand.

I also use a coarse sponge called a stipple sponge for imitating a three-day beard on the

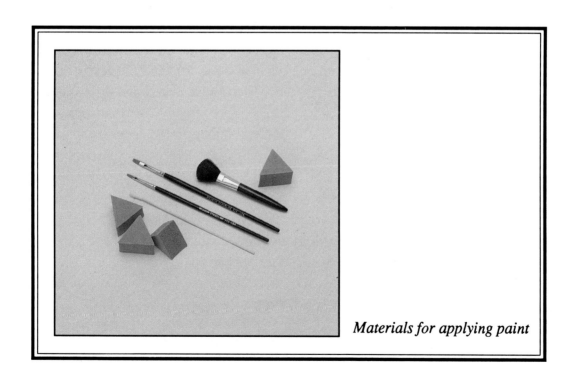

Materials for applying paint

pirate and hobo clown. A small piece of paper towel dipped in the paint can be used to create a similar effect.

Cotton pads can also be used to apply large amounts of paint to the face. The advantage of cotton pads is that you can discard the pads after use, making them more sanitary and saving you time in cleanup. The disadvantage is that cotton may leave some fuzz on the child's face. Make sure to use cotton pads and not cotton balls because the balls come apart too easily.

Container of Water
You will need water to moisten your paints and to clean your brushes and sponges. Use a small container of water (a plastic cup works fine) to work with as you paint and a larger container to hold clean water. When the water in the small container becomes murky, dump it out and replace it with clean water. Some painters like to use opaque containers so the murky water cannot be seen. If you worry about hygiene add a few drops of alcohol to your water.

Baby Wipes
Baby wipes are used for cleaning brushes, kid's dirty faces, partially painted faces of kids who changed their minds, your hands, mistakes, your working surface, and just about anything that needs a sparkling touch. I never leave home without them and neither should you! A small terry cloth towel is a good companion to your baby wipes. Use it in your lap to protect your clothes from the paint. Be careful not to place baby wipes or anything wet on fine furniture or table cloths. Keep a plastic bag to use as a surface.

Headbands and Hair Clips
Headbands, hair clips, and bobby pins serve to keep hair away from a child's face while it is being painted. They're especially nice on windy days when hair is less controllable.

Towel
You may want to put a towel or cape over the children to keep from dripping paint on their clothes. You can use an ordinary towel or a plastic shampoo cape sold at beauty supply stores.

Even though paint will wash out of clothing, the children or their parents may not want them to walk around all day with spotted clothes. If some paint does get on clothes, you can easily wash it off with a paper towel or baby wipe while it's still wet.

Blushes
I used to use the tip of my finger dipped in red paint as blush for all of the designs that required it. Then I discovered that a powder blush was much more effective. I tried some of the commercial brands found at the local drugstore, but none of them seemed as bright or as easy to apply as I wanted them to be. I'm currently using one designed for theatrical use that is manufactured by Kryolan. The color I use is called Youth Red. Ask your dealer or write to me for its availability (see appendix). If you decide to go with a store brand, choose the brightest red or pink you can find.

Eye Shadow, Mascara and Color Hair Spray
I use these items only if time permits or if I'm

working with teenagers and adults. If you are charging a "per face" fee for your service, the hair spray works as an extra incentive for a sale. At a carnival, fair, or fundraiser, adults and teenagers who normally wouldn't care to have their faces painted will go for a funky streak of hair color.

Glitter

You can add sparkle and shine to the face with glitter. Many people prefer not to use glitter. They fear it may get into a child's eye and cause an injury. I have never had a problem with it, because I apply it very carefully and in minimum amounts, and I never put glitter on the eyelids or lips! But the fear is not unfounded, especially if you are using the wrong kind of glitter. I use an ultra thin glitter called "crystalline" which, unlike the regular glitter found at craft stores, is not metallic. Instead, it is made of plastic.

The glitter is easily applied to the face using a moistened finger. The thinness of the glitter allows it to stick well to the paint without flaking. The plastic, unlike the metal, is also non-irritating.

At one time I used a variety of colors; but later on I found that the crystalline—a clear, transparent, prismatic color—is all I needed. It takes on the color of any paint it is applied to. Once again, you may check with you local dealer or write to me directly for its availability.

To be safe, never use glitter around the eyes or on the lips and do not use glue.

MIRROR

The biggest satisfaction that comes from face painting is watching the expressions on children's faces as they look at themselves in the mirror. Don't waste this precious moment with a tiny pocket mirror. Use one that is clear and sturdy. Wipe it off as often as needed and, to avoid scratches, make a cover or case to carry it in.

One thing I like to do is glue a picture of a monkey or a funny-looking creature on the back of the mirror. It's fun to ask the children if they'd like to see how they look. Flipping the mirror over, I show them the funny side. It always gets a laugh. Recently, while shopping at a local mall, I found a mirror that already had a built-in frame on the back side. This works even better as I can change the picture from time to time.

When working a big crowd for long hours, such as at a carnival or fair, a large mirror on a stand, or even a table top mirror, will add a lot to your face painting experience. Besides the fact that the children truly enjoy looking at themselves, it can serve as an interesting distraction for the other children waiting their turn.

When there are a large number of children waiting, I give each child a number, which I paint directly on their hands or on a sticker to be affixed to a blouse, shirt or sweater. This assures that each child is taken care of in order.

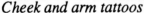
Cheek and arm tattoos

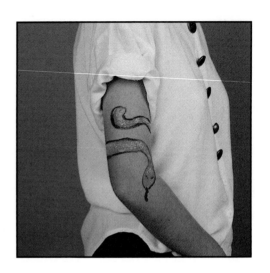

Face painting is a fun and colorful pastime and hobby. Decorate your mirror accordingly. The back of a wooden mirror is a perfect place to advertise yourself using your logo, name, or even your picture. For repeat engagements, it is important that the client remember your name.

Fake Blood

Fake blood is a red colored paint commonly sold in a toothpaste-like tube. It is good when creating cuts, bruises, and special monster effects. Believe me, older kids (especially boys) love gory things! This is also an optional item on your list since you can use watered down red to create a similar effect.

Carrying Case

Finally, you will need a carrying case for all your materials. A decorated lunchbox or fishing tackle box works very well. Actually, any brightly decorated box or container big enough to hold all of your supplies will do. I prefer one with a good handle. Tool boxes, especially the ones with a tray, are excellent.

Because face painting is a full-time job for me, I have designed a carrying case to fit my specific needs. My case is red with a yellow handle, which matches my costume, and is made out of a heavy plastic. Since I use a large quantity of paints in a short time, I put my paints in one oz. containers such as the plastic ones used to hold silver dollars and other large coins. You may purchase these containers from a coin dealer or an art supply store. I refill these containers as they get low and they hold up for a long time. To save me time as I set up and pack up, all the container tops are labeled with a permanent magic marker. Periodically it is important to give your case an overhaul—clean and arrange everything to make it look neat. The appearance of your equipment is important because it reflects on your character and work.

For a while, I carried the containers of paint loose in the case. This used to annoy me because they would rattle in the case. To solve the problem, I purchased a piece of foam which I cut up to fit the inside of the case. I also cut out enough spaces in the foam to fit each container—plus a place for the sponges, brushes, and glitter. The mirror, baby towels, and a small terry cloth lay neatly on top of it all.

Now that you know what materials you will need, you are ready to start your adventure into the wonderful world of face painting. Have fun.

PREPARING THE FACE

For best results you should start with a completely clean face. Since face painting is often done at parties, fairs, and other social gatherings, the face you will be painting will often be smudged with candy, food, or dirt. Wipe the face clean with a baby wipe before you apply any paint.

At times young ladies and women with cosmetic makeup will request a face. If they have used a lot of makeup or dark rich colors that may affect your design you can wipe it off. If their makeup is minimal and will not affect your design, just paint over it.

Long hair can get in the way. Because it is bothersome to hold it up out of the way., I use a headband or hair clips to keep hair off the face and away from the paint until the makeup dries.

MIXING COLORS

The most commonly available paint colors are white, red, blue, yellow, and black. Additional colors can be created by mixing a pair of these colors together. To keep all of your paints clean, mix the colors together in a separate little container or dish.

BLUE + YELLOW = GREEN

YELLOW + RED = ORANGE

RED + BLUE = PURPLE

RED + WHITE = PINK

RED + BLACK = BROWN

BLACK + WHITE = GRAY

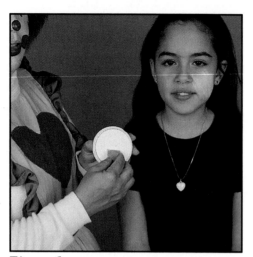

Figure 1

Figure 2

APPLYING FOUNDATION COLORS

Several of the faces described in this book require covering the entire face with a foundation or base coat of paint upon which to build. Clowns use either a white, pink, or flesh-color base. A green base is used on the Ninja Turtles, witches, and some monsters. A light gray is also used on some of the scary faces.

Some face painters prefer to use a white base coat on almost all the faces they make. Where a base coat is not specifically given in the instructions, you can usually use a white base if you wish. Applying the extra coat of paint takes longer but produces a very sharp looking facial design that stands out.

Here's how to apply a white base coat. The same procedure applies to any base color.

Start with a clean face. If necessary clean the child's face with a baby wipe.

The base color is applied to the face with a moistened sponge or cotton pad (Figure 1). Soak the sponge in warm water then gently squeeze out some of the water. You want the sponge to be damp, not dripping wet. The water fills the pore spaces in the sponge, making cleanup easier and conserving paint. Use warm water if at all possible. You don't want the child screaming with shock after applying a cold wet sponge to the face. If warm water is not available, at least prepare the child by warning that the sponge will be cold.

Now dip the sponge into the white paint. Get a good amount of paint on the sponge, but not so much that it's dripping wet. Gradually cover the entire face with the paint. Cover all the skin up to the hairline and

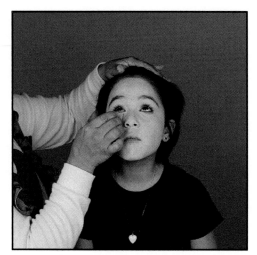

Figure 4

Figure 3

Figure 5

along the sideburns but keep the paint out of the hair as much as possible (Figure 2). Use as much paint as needed but not so much that it is caked on the face when dry.

You may also cover the eyelids with paint. Have the child relax and close her eyes without squinting. If she can't keep from squinting, tell her to relax and pretend she is sleeping. This should help. gently brush the sponge downward over the eyelids (Figure 3). Have the child look up to cover under her eyes (Figure 4). Use your free hand to steady her head.

Cover the entire face down to the chin. Cover the chin and jaw, ending with an even line just underneath the jaw. Coat the face as evenly as possible (Figure 5). If you use too much paint this may produce a streaky appearance. Patting the sponge gently on the face will help even out the paint.

Wait thirty seconds for the paint to dry com-pletely before applying any overlying colors. Fanning the face will help dry the paint faster.

APPLYING LINES

Full face foundation and heavy shading are best applied with sponges. Lines and fine designs are applied with brushes. Cotton swabs can also be used. Most face designs require the use of some lines. Use a thin brush for fine lines and thicker brushes for coarse lines and markings. Paint takes a minute or so to dry on the face. Before it dries it can mix and smear. Be careful that neither the child nor you accidentally touches the face until the paint is dry. Let each color dry before adding another color to avoid unintentionally mixing the colors on the face and producing a third unwanted color.

Thin lines can be applied with a narrow brush. Medium lines require a thicker brush or a Q-tip. Thick lines can be applied with a thick brush or your finger tip.

Use plenty of paint on the brush but not so much that it becomes messy or drippy. Brushes can be washed off in a cup of water. Rinse the paint off the brush before applying another color. Q-tips don't rinse well so use a new one for each color.

For best results when painting lines, use long, even strokes rather than short choppy strokes. If you make a mistake, simply wipe off the paint with a wet paper towel or baby wipe and try again.

Kids are naturally wiggly. Encouraging them to hold still will help but won't totally prevent smears from happening. To reduce movement as you paint, place your free hand on top of the child's head or under the chin. You may also steady your painting hand by resting your little finger against the side of the child's head as you paint fine detail. Your hand will be much less likely to wander when you use this technique

EYES

Be very careful when applying paint around the eyes. When you paint people's faces, be sure to tell them to hold still. As a precaution when you paint near the eyes have the children keep their eyes closed.

For many of the faces pictured in this book I have applied paint close to the eyes. A sudden twist of a child's head can cause you to put paint where it wasn't intended. To avoid getting paint in the eyes or poking someone with the brush, you may want to avoid painting near the eyes. It is also helpful if you hold the child's head steady with your free hand as you apply paint near the eyes.

The skin around the eye is delicate, so apply paint with gentle strokes. Generally, I would recommend that you avoid coloring the eyelids unless you cover them with a sponge when applying a base coat over the entire face.

Do not use glitter near or around the eyes. Even one tiny piece in the eye can cause extreme discomfort.

ADHESIVES

Do not use glues that are not specifically made for the face or skin. Some people use ordinary household glue to stick on sequins (small glass beads) and glitter. This type of glue can be difficult to remove and may cause irritation, a rash, or an allergic reaction.

There are several types of adhesive that are made especially for use on the skin. Eyelash adhesive is one and is available in most drug stores. Liquid latex or spirit gum can also be used, but some people are allergic to these so use them with caution.

Adhesives are not really necessary for face painting. Glitter and even sequins will adhere to the face through the holding power of the paint itself. After the paint has been applied to the face, just stick the glitter directly onto it. When you wash off the paint, the glitter comes off too. What could be easier?

SANITATION

Since there are occasions in which you may paint several faces at a single sitting, you should keep your equipment as sanitary as possible. Always wash your brushes and sponges before you use them. Dishwashing liquid works well. And always rinse your brushes and sponges thoroughly after painting each face.

As an extra precaution I would recommend that you use at least two sets of brushes and sponges. After using one set of brushes, rinse them off thoroughly and then soak them in a small container with a 50-50 mixture of water and rubbing alcohol. This will help keep the brushes sterile. While one set of brushes is soaking, use the other set. Alternate brushes for each face you paint. After the brushes have soaked, rinse the alcohol mixture off with clean water before dipping them back into the paint.

The most sanitary method would be to use cotton swabs and cotton pads in place of brushes and sponges. Once they have been used they are discarded so that each face begins with unused materials. Also, cleanup is easier since you don't have to wash out any brushes.

However, since cotton swabs can't produce fine even lines like a brush can, you may consider using a combination of alcohol, brushes, sponges, and cotton swabs and pads. Ordinary care, plus the use of the alcohol solution, should be adequate for all sanatition needs.

REMOVING PAINT

Removing water-soluble paint is easy. Just use ordinary soap and water.

If the paint gets on your clothes, wash it out with laundry detergent along with your regular wash. Some colors may be a little stubborn so it is advisable to wipe off as much spilled paint as possible from the clothing before it dries.

Be sure to tell the children and their parents that the paint will wash off with soap and water. Many parents may assume that the paint, like theatrical and cosmetic makeups, will need to be removed with cold cream or other makeup removers. Explaining to parents that the paints you use are water-soluble and will easily wash off will relieve their apprehensions and allow many children the opportunity to be painted.

Some children may refuse to be painted, thinking that the paint, like house paint, will not come off. You can show them how easily the paint washes off by applying some to your own arm and then washing it off with a wet towel or baby wipe.

Kitten

The kitten is one of the simplest of all the face painting designs and the quickest to make. It is great for babies, wigglers, squinters, and children who are not too sure about having their faces painted. Once you know how to make the kitten, you can easily create the tiger, werewolf, and other animals simply by changing the colors, the directions of the stripes, or the size of the spots.

Begin by applying rouge to the cheeks. Using black or brown, paint a half-circle on the tip of the nose, and three whiskers on each cheek (Figure 6). In the space between the nose and upper lip, draw a series of small dots. To draw the cat's eyes, begin at the upper part of the nose and follow the shape of the eye going up and around, ending at the outside of the eye as shown in Figure 7.

In older children or adults, you may want to color the tips of the eye design in order to create a more dramatic effect. The eyes look good in brown, black, green, white, blue, or any metallic color. To finish, draw a small, round heart in the center of the lips, using red or pink for a girl kitty, and black or brown for a boy kitty. Apply glitter to the nose and cheeks.

Figure 6

Figure 7

TIGER

To create the tiger, first apply orange, brown, or yellow to the cheeks and to the area between the upper lip and nose (Figure 8). Using black or brown, draw a half-circle on the nose, whiskers on the cheeks, and a series of dots above the upper lip (Figure 9). Draw cat eyes as in the kitty, and shade in the outside edge a little bit (Figure 10).

Starting in the middle of the forehead, proceed to draw lines on the face to resemble a tiger's fur (Figure 11). Go around the face using your main color, then repeat using black or brown. draw two teeth (fangs) at the corners of the lips. For variations, use shorter or longer lines. You can also experiment by zigzagging the lines or using spots..

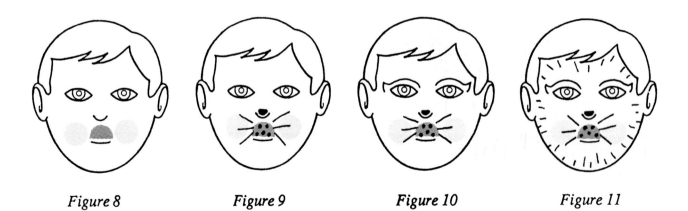

Figure 8   Figure 9   Figure 10   Figure 11

Bunny

The bunny is one of the cutest face designs, and definitely my favorite for small children. In my opinion, if you are face painting at a birthday party and can convince the young birthday child to be a bunny, it will guarantee you a return engagement. Bunnies are cuddly and cute, and the adults, as well as the children, just love them.

First apply either rouge or pink paint above the eyebrows, to the cheeks, and tip of the nose (Figure 12). Starting on the side of the nose, draw two long white half-circles over the tops of the eyes (Figure 13).

Picking up from where you started, draw a circular line down around the cheeks and end on the chin. Repeat on the other side (Figure 14). Add a few bunny hairs, whiskers and dots above the upper lip and nose. Plant two small teeth on the bottom lip for a great finishing touch (Figure 15).

If you know how to make animals and other figures out of balloons you could make a set of bunny ears. A set of bunny balloon ears adds a powerful finishing touch to the design.

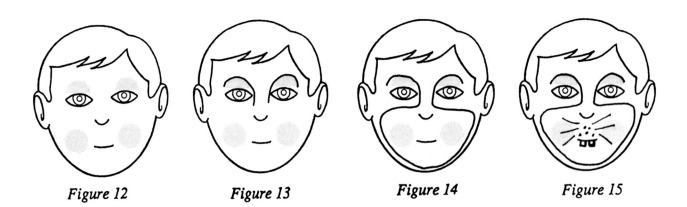

Figure 12   *Figure 13*   *Figure 14*   *Figure 15*

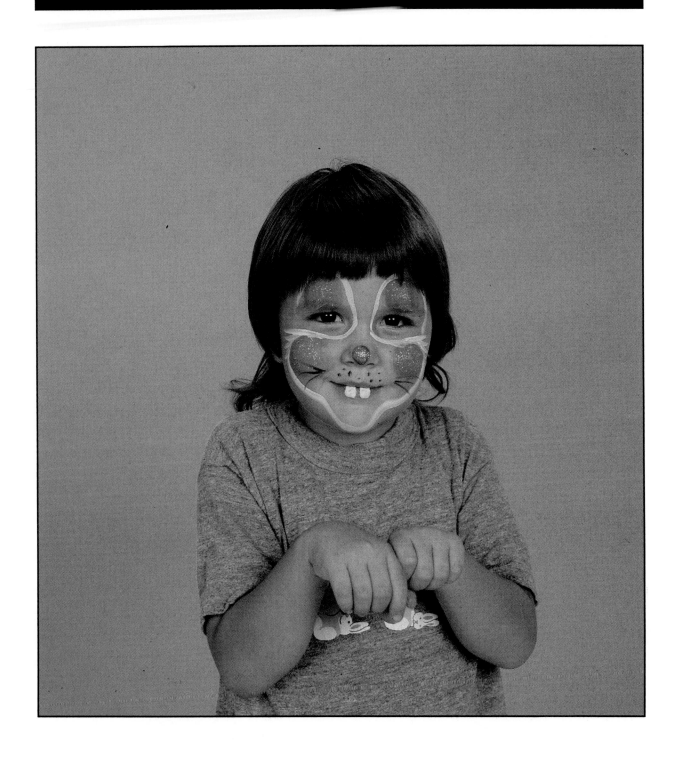

Puppy

Like the bunny, the puppy is a good choice for small children or when you are short of time. Its simplicity makes it fast and easy. Like the bunny, parents love the design because children look adorable as puppies.

Apply white around the mouth and above the eyebrows (Figure 16). Use blush on cheeks. With black, draw in the nose and outline the eyebrows and the mouth (Figure 17). Color the bottom lip only, and draw a series of dots on the area above the lips. For variations, add spots, draw a tongue sticking out from the corner of the lips, color around one eye in black, or make white and black spots to make a dalmatian.

Figure 16

Figure 17

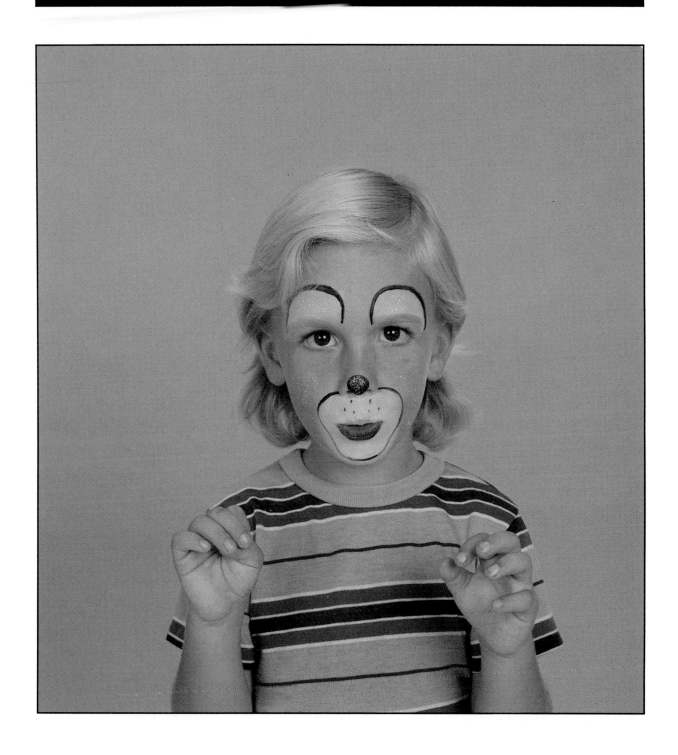

Zebra

The Zebra is very simple and quick to make. Because it requires more paint, it is best for older kids.

Start by applying white to the face, using a sponge moistened in water. Using black, draw a circle on the tip of the nose and catlike eyes (Figure 18). Divide the face with a line from the top of the forehead to the chin (Figure 19). Draw the rest of the lines around the face (Figure 20). Color the lips in black.

Figure 18

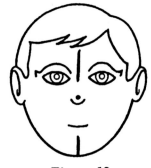

Figure 19

Figure 20

Butterfly

If done correctly the butterfly is one of the most beautiful designs. It is best for older girls and adults because it requires paint around the eyes.

It is time-consuming, so it is best not to attempt this design if a large number of people want to have their faces painted. Draw the outline of the butterfly wings, starting with the cat eyes and extending them to the tip of the mouth (figure 22). Using very gentle strokes, start coloring the wings in a featherlike motion. Use three different colors, almost blending them together (Study the picture.)

Draw the butterfly body in the middle of the nose by drawing a small circle for the head and a larger oval for the body. Add two antennae to the head, ending with a curl in the forehead (figure 21). Paint lips pink or red, except on boys.

Study the photograph to get ideas on the different designs you can create by adding dots and lines to the wings.

The butterfly gives you a chance to get creative.

Figure 21

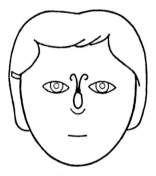

Figure 22

FANTASY FACES

Flower

The flower is beautiful on older girls, who absolutely love the design! It is a good design to offer after a butterfly, which it complements.

Use your imagination and creativity for mixing and matching the colors and shapes of the petals. The possibilities are endless.

Apply blush to the cheeks. Draw a circle around one eye (Figure 23). In this example I've colored the center of the circle yellow. On younger children, use commercial eye shadow. Draw petals around the circle (Figure 24) and color them in. For a special effect, outline the petals in a different color. Draw the stem, circling the face (Figure 25) and add leaves. Finish by painting the lips.

Figure 23

Figure 24

Figure 25

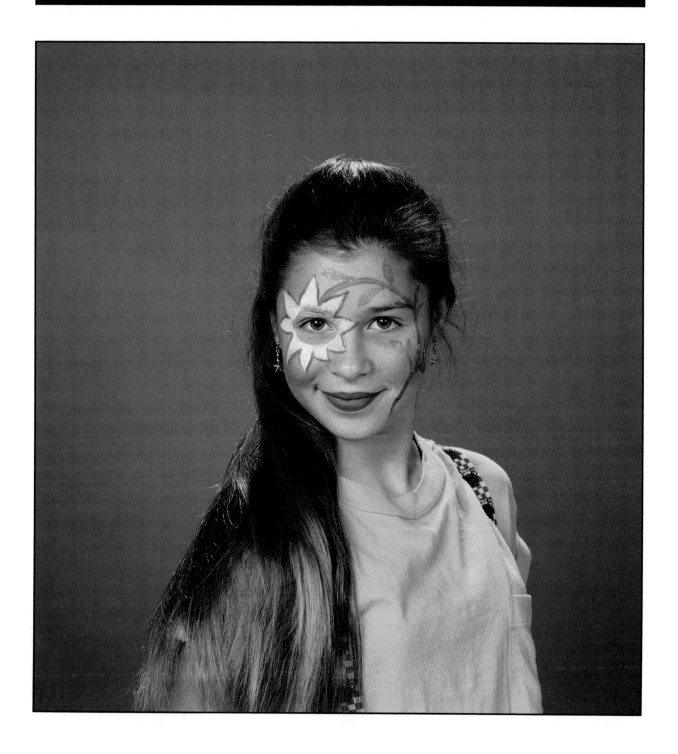

Rock Star

This design is popular with older children, both male and female. It looks best in black, white, purple, and metallic colors. Start by painting one side of the face white, using a moist sponge. Leave space around the eye for a star and make a thunderbolt on the opposite cheek (Figure 26).

Using a moist sponge, color the other half of the face black (Figure 27). Draw a straight black line directly down the center of the face. Color in the star on the eye, and outline the rest of the face (Figure 28). Use a baby wipe if you need to erase mistakes. Finish by coloring the lips in either red or purple.

Figure 26

Figure 27

Figure 28

Mardi Gras Girl

This is one of my favorite designs. However, because there is paint on the eyelid, I recommend it only for older girls. This design is also popular with adults.

Begin by applying rouge and lipstick (Figure 29). The rest of the design is done entirely around the eyes.

For the eye designs, any combination of colors will do, so I try to match the color of the person's eyes or clothes. For a dramatic effect, I like to use metallic colors outlined with black. Use your imagination.

Starting at the corner of the eye, draw the designs and shade in with various colors (Figure 30). Study the picture on the right to get ideas on the different designs you can create by combining the shape and size of the extending lines. Use your imagination. You can dress this design up a bit by adding a thunderbolt or star on the cheek.

Figure 29

Figure 30

Rainbowland Princess

The princess is, without a doubt, one of my favorite designs and the favorite of girls three to thirteen years of age. I call this design the Rainbowland Princess because of all the beautiful colors, or the Fairy Princess, because it looks so beautiful.

Older girls can be called Rainbow Queens, but the design is basically the same. The pattern, as you will see, is very symmetrical. By changing the main shape from a heart to a diamond, a flower, or a star, and by combining the colors to match eyes or clothes, you can do a hundred princesses and none of them will be exactly the same. This is the beauty of this design.

Apply blush to cheeks and lipstick to the lips (Figure 31). Start by drawing a star, heart, diamond, or flower in the middle of the child's forehead (Figure 32). One of these will be the main shape of the headband. Using dots and a combination of the main shape, form a complete headband across the forehead (Figure 33).

Now draw in the eye design starting from the corner of the eyes. Use a combination of lines and colors to create a design around the eyes. Study the picture on the following page. As you practice making the princess, you will have fun creating original designs of your own.

Figure 31

Figure 32

Figure 33

Queens

Many times you will encounter little girls with bangs who will want to be princesses. Because of the hair covering the forehead, drawing the headband will not be practical.

My solution is to make them queens, doing the design *under* the eyes.

This design looks best if you try to match your paints to the color of their clothes, eyes and hair.

First, apply blush to the cheeks and color the lips (Figure 34). Draw a heart, flower or star on the middle of the forehead and something to match at the corner of the eyes. (Figure 35).

Complete the design by making two half-circles under the eyes, using dots of different colors (Figure 36).

Study the photograph to stimulate your imagination. As with the princesses the possibilities for this design are endless.

Figure 34

Figure 35

Figure 36

Space Woman

This is a beautiful and sophisticated design for older girls and adults. It also gives you a great opportunity to be creative and a chance to use metallic colors if you have them available. Small children won't appreciate this design as much as older ones will.

Apply heavy blush to the cheeks. Starting at the very top of the nose, draw cat-like eyes (Figure 37). This will be your guideline for the rest of the face design. Add the eyebrow designs and paint them in different shades of color. (Figure 38).

Draw a triangle, star, or dot in the middle of the forehead and chin (Figure 39). Using a color that matches the color of the clothes and facial designs, paint the lips (Figure 40). Adding false eyelashes is optional.

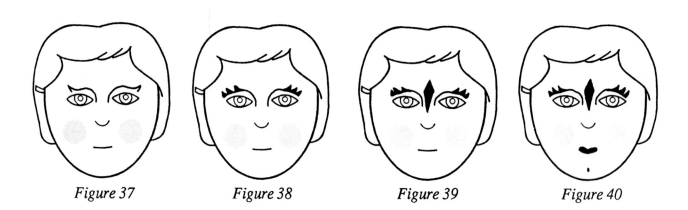

Figure 37   Figure 38   Figure 39   Figure 40

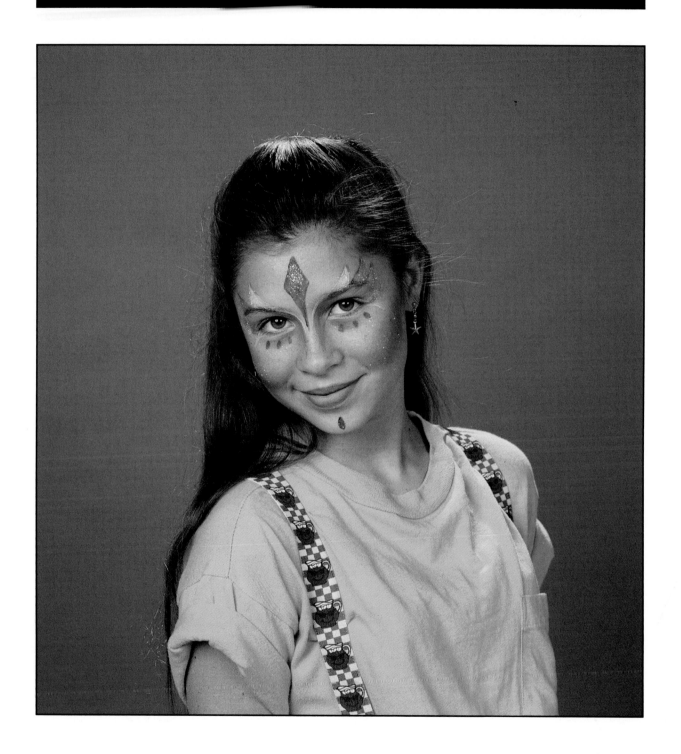

Mermaid

Like the Princess and the Queens, the Mermaid is very popular with girls of all ages. The final look is beautiful on any girl.

First, apply blush to the cheeks and paint the lips. Make a headband in a V shape and color it in (Figure 41). Outline the headband in a different color. On the headband, you can now draw either pearls, little fish, shells, or anything else related to the sea (Figure 42).

On the outside edges of the eyes. add a few lines—either straight or curled—to represent seaweeds (Figure 43). The Mermaid is a very simple design and little girls love it!

Figure 41

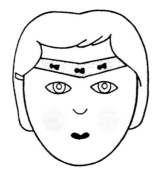

Figure 42

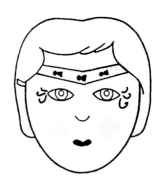

Figure 43

Indian Warrior and Princess

The Indian warrior and princess are very simple and fast designs. The key is always to start at the center of the face and whatever you do on one side, do again on the other.

The Indian warrior design is the simplest of the two. Using any color you choose, draw a line from the tip of the nose to the beginning of the forehead. Draw one straight line emanating from the outside edge of each eye, an open triangle on the cheeks, and a straight line in the middle of the chin. This will establish your basic design (Figure 44).

Now all you need to do is add in lines of different colors, parallel to the ones already there. See the completed warrior on the next page. By changing the colors and shape or length of the lines, you will be able to create many different designs.

The Indian princess has a very similar design. Put a diamond or triangle in the center of her forehead. Add an open triangle to the outside edge of each cheek (Figure 45). This is the basic design for the princess. Add in the remaining lines. Use the picture on the following page as a guide. Add lipstick and blush to the princess for the finishing touch.

Figure 44

Figure 45

Whiteface Clown

I love to create faces of funny characters, especially clown faces. By varying the features of the clown face, you can create hundreds of different designs. Clown faces, however, are one of the most time-consuming designs.

The first clown face I will show you is called a Whiteface. The name comes from the fact that the entire face is coated with white makeup. Other colors used to outline or enhance facial features are then applied over the white.

Using a moist sponge, apply white paint over the entire face (see pages 16 and 17). Make sure the face is completely covered. Go slowly around the eye area, reassuring the child that you will not get any paint into the eyes. To get under the eye, have the

child look up to the ceiling. Once the white paint has dried, apply rouge on the cheeks. With red, draw a circle for a nose (Figure 46). The easiest and most common mouth on a clown is constructed by painting only the bottom lip and adding two circles at each side of the mouth (Figure 47).

The next step is to add a design around the eye area. For the clown pictured here, I painted two lines extending out from the top and bottom of each eye. A design coming from the outside edge of each eye is added.

The shape of the eyebrows can be anything from a straight line to a half circle or a triangle (Figure 48). Hearts, balloons, stars, or any other designs on the cheeks are optional.

Figure 46

Figure 47

Figure 48

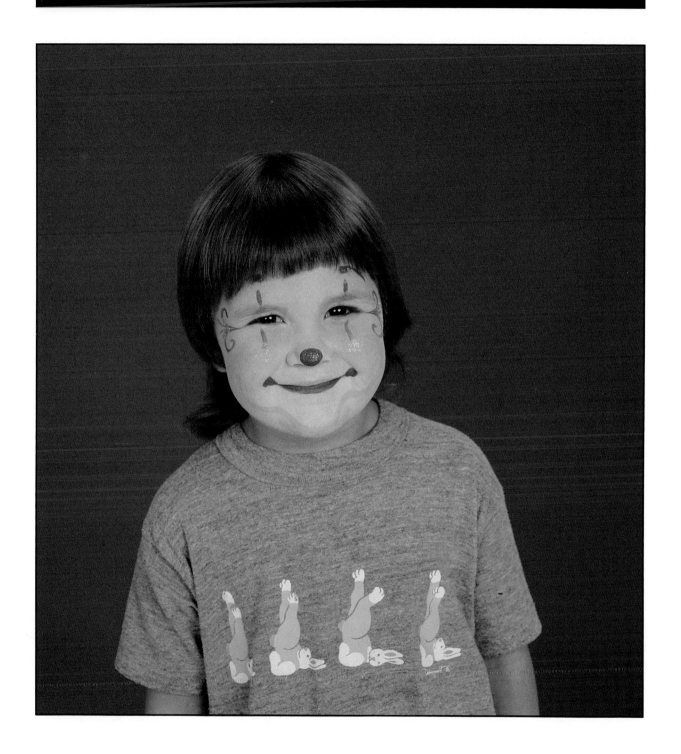

Auguste Clown

In contrast to the Whiteface, the Auguste (pronounced "aw-goost") has a pink or flesh colored base. Other colors are added for the facial features. White is usually used around the eyes and the mouth.

In this example, I use the natural skin color as the base. But if you like, you could cover the entire face, except the eye and mouth area, with a pink color. It takes more time to create the face this way, but it makes a more colorful clown.

Using the moist sponge, apply white around the mouth and around the eye area (Figure 49). Apply rouge around the outside edge of the white mouth. Draw a red nose (Figure 50). Using any color that matches the color of the eyes or clothes, outline the mouth area and draw the eyebrows (Figure 51). If the clown is a girl, use red to paint the smile on the lips; if a boy, use black. Finish the eye design by drawing lines under the eyes (Figure 52).

As with the Whiteface clown, you can vary the size and shape of the Auguste's features to create many different looking faces.

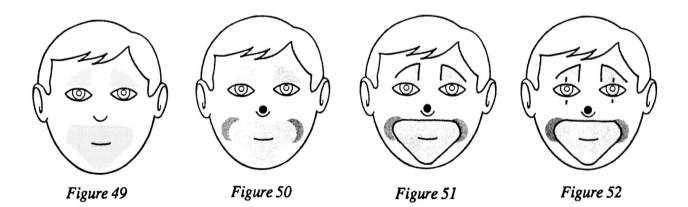

Figure 49 *Figure 50* *Figure 51* *Figure 52*

Hobo Clown

The Hobo Clown depicts a comical street person. The base color is pink or flesh. White is used around the eyes and mouth. Begin by applying white around the mouth and eye area (Figure 53). Add a little rouge to the cheeks and color the end of the nose (Figure 54).

Using black, draw eyebrows. The best type of eyebrows for the hobo are the ones with a slant that will give the face a sad expression.

Still using black, draw a small smile on the bottom lip only and a tear coming out of each eye (Figure 55). Using a napkin or a stipple sponge dipped in black paint, pat gently around the chin and jaw to produce the stubbly appearance of a three-day-old beard.

Figure 53

Figure 54

Figure 55

Mime

The Mime is a more elegant type of Whiteface clown. The Mime clown, unlike other clowns, uses less outlandish designs and features, resulting in a very pleasing looking face. The only colors used are white, black, and red.

Cover the face with white paint. When the paint has dried, apply a small amount of blush to the cheeks (Figure 56). Draw a small circle on the nose (op-tional) and paint the lips as a woman would when applying lipstick (Figure 57). Using black, draw a circle around the entire face enclosing the white. Draw a solid triangle-like shape under each eye and lines emanating from the corner of the eyes. Add a set of dainty eyebrows and the forehead design (Figure 58).

Figure 56

Figure 57

Figure 58

Goofy Person

This silly design is sometimes referred to as the nerd. But I prefer to call it a goofy person and have fun with it. Remember, always laugh with the kids and not at them!

Begin by applying a little blush to the cheeks (Figure 59). Draw two circles around the eyes and connect them at the nose to look like glasses (Figure 60). Add freckles, a couple of teeth on the bottom lip, and slanted eyebrows (Figure 61). This design is very simple and lots of fun.

Figure 59

Figure 60

Figure 61

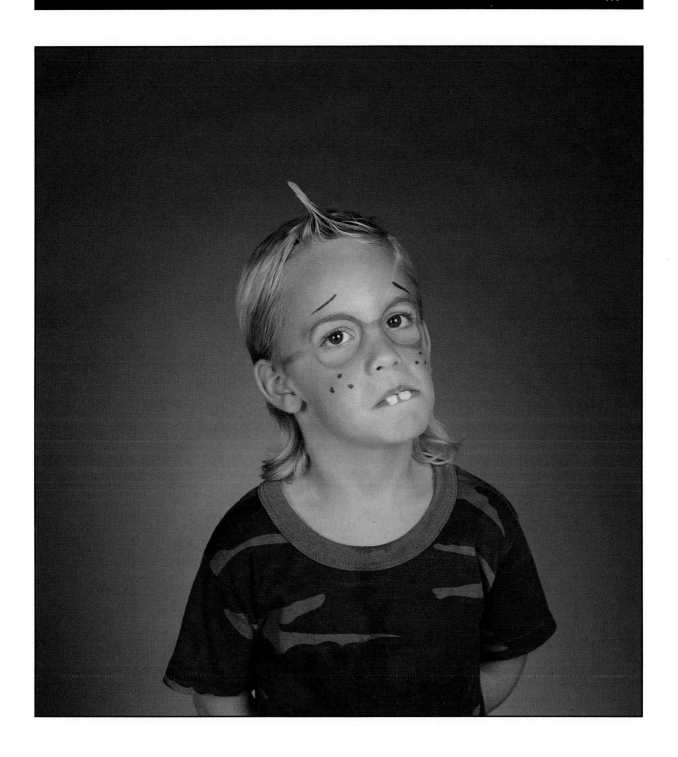

Mickey and Minnie Mouse

Mickey is a character whose popularity will never fade and is one of my most requested designs at birthday parties. Mickey looks great on little ones, but because it requires covering the entire face with white, it takes a little longer and is a little harder than most of the other faces.

Apply white on the face in the form of a round heart (Figure 62). Apply blush to the cheeks (Figure 63). Using black, draw a circle for a nose and outline the white face. Draw two small eyebrows (Figure 64).

For Mickey, color the lips with black paint. For Minnie's mouth, use red. The differences between Minnie and Mickey are in the eyebrows and the color of the lips. Minnie has eyelashes, Mickey a single eyebrow.

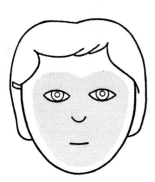

Figure 62

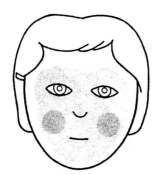

Figure 63

Figure 64

Spiderman

At first glance, Spiderman looks difficult, but the design is actually very easy and fast because it uses only two colors.

Begin by drawing a spider in the middle of the nose. Do so by drawing a small dot and adding a larger oval for the body (Figure 65). Make sure you draw eight legs, otherwise the children will tell you that it's not a spider, it's a roach.

Draw cat-like eyes. In red, draw a circle around the whole face and divide it as you would a pie (Figure 66). Connect the lines using half-circles beginning in the middle of the forehead. A little farther apart, draw a second set of half circles connecting the lines around the face (Figure 67). Color lips in blue (optional).

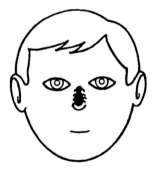

Figure 65

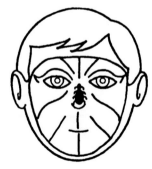

Figure 66

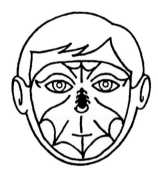

Figure 67

Wonder Woman

For Wonder Woman, you need to have a child who does not have bangs, as the design is done completely on the forehead.

Apply rouge and lipstick (Figure 68). Draw a white star in the middle of the forehead. The easiest way to make the star is to first draw a triangle. Add another triangle upside down on top of the first one. Using blue, make a headband emanating from the star (Figure 69). That's all...simple, fast, and it looks great!

Figure 68

Figure 69

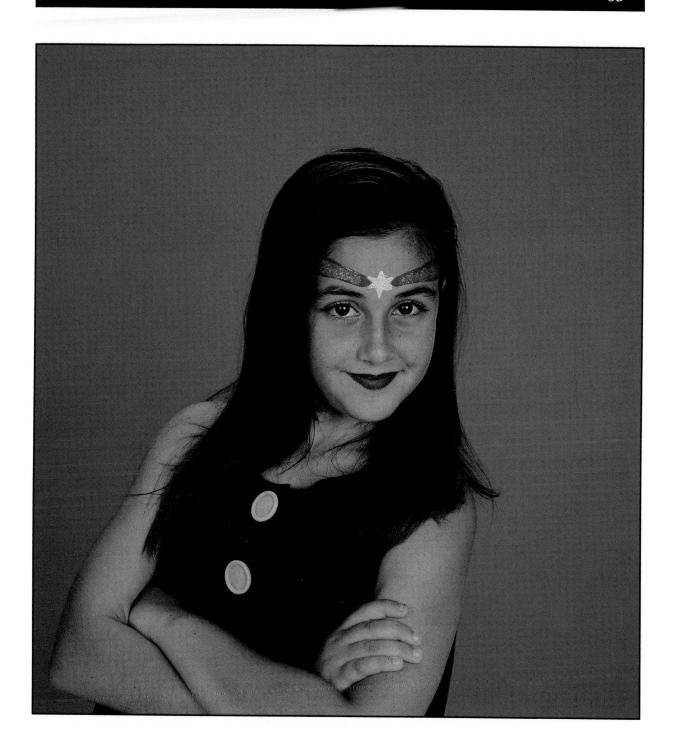

Batman and Batwoman

Batman is one of the most popular designs. Unfortunately, it is not as easy to do as many of the others and is definitely more time-consuming. It will take a little practice, but in time, you will learn to speed it up.

Begin by practicing the outline of the bat's mask on a piece of paper. When applying the design to a face, the best way to do it is by starting in the middle of the forehead with a small loop. Then draw the outline on one side of the face and repeat it on the other side (Figure 70). with practice, you will be able to do this in a matter of seconds.

Now draw two circles around the eyes (Figure 71). the next step, which is the time consuming one, is to color in the mask in black. This is the only time when I recommend putting a lot of paint on the brush. Also, make the strokes go in the same direction so the finished product won't look blotchy. Outline the mask using yellow or blue (Figure 72).

Batwoman is basically the same design except that I use pastel colors like pink or light blue.

Figure 70

Figure 71

Figure 72

Ninja Turtle

As with Batman, the Ninja Turtles are a very popular design. It's not one of my favorites because it is time-consuming, but it is fun to see the kid's reaction when I'm finished, and that alone makes it worthwhile.

With a moist sponge, cover the face with green paint, leaving the eye area open (Figure 73). Learn the names of the Ninja Turtle characters and the colors on the headbands matching each character: Donatello (purple), Michaelangelo (orange), Leonardo (blue), Raphael (red). Ask the child which one he would like to be. Then, taking the corresponding color, draw a headband across the eyes (Figure 74). As with Batman, before coloring in the headband, draw two circles around the eyes. To finish, use dark green or black to paint a smile (Figure 75).

Figure 73

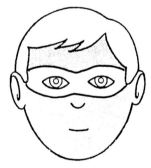

Figure 74

Figure 75

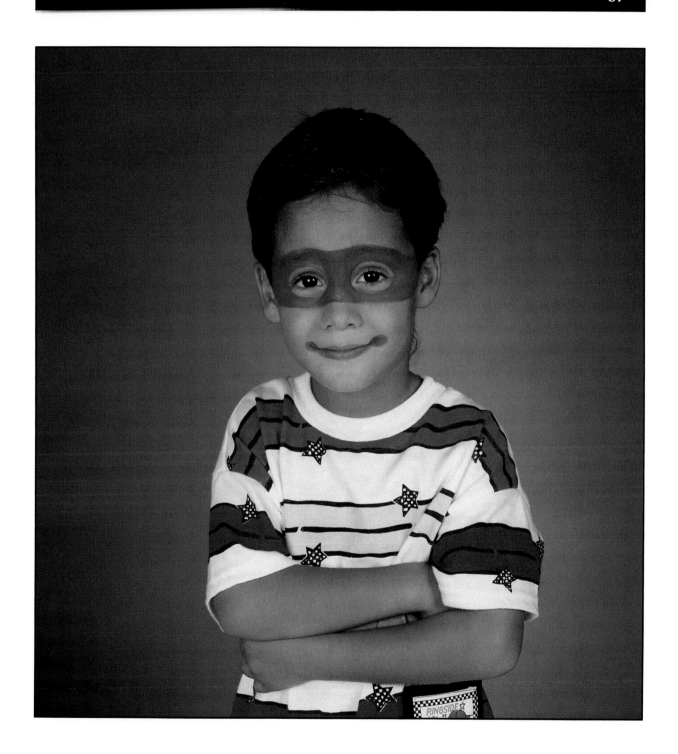

Captain Crook the Pirate

Most of the face in this section are more complex than average because of the shading involved and because most of them require covering the entire face with paint. Older children appreciate these designs more than the younger ones do. A small bottle of fake blood (available at novelty and toy stores) will create wonderful effects. These designs are a little on the morbid side, but kids really get a kick out of them!

The pirate is the simplest of the designs in this section. It makes a good, easy design for the younger kids.

Apply blush to cheeks (Figure 76). Using black or brown, draw a moustache with curly ends and a small beard (Figure 77). Draw a circle around one eye and color it in. Add the strap that would hold an eye patch (Figure 78).

Darken in the other eyebrow if necessary. Using a stipple sponge, or a paper napkin dipped lightly in black or brown, pat the paint around the cheeks to produce the appearance of a three-day-old beard.

For dramatic effect, add a scar or wound (see page 84).

Figure 76

Figure 77

Figure 78

Vampire

The vampire is the most popular of the scary designs and one of the simplest. The following steps are used to turn a boy into Dracula and a girl into Vampira.

Start by covering the entire face with white or a very light gray paint as was done for the clowns. Apply it with a sponge moistened with water.

Mix some black paint with white to form a medium gray. Use a sponge to apply the gray mixture, and shade in the sides of the nose, the cheeks, and the area below the eyes as shown in Figure 79.

With black, draw the eyebrows in a triangle shape to create a dramatic expression on the face. Draw Dracula's hairline, and color it in (Figure 80).

Paint lips in black or purple and add two downward protruding fangs in the corners of the mouth (Figure 81).

For a dramatic effect, add a little blood to the teeth or mouth.

Figure 79

Figure 80

Figure 81

Frankenstein's Monster

Frankenstein's Monster is also a very popular monster face. It can be created with a base coat of green like the Ninja Turtle.

Shade in around the eyes to give a sunken, spooky look. Darken the eyebrows (Figure 82). Now all you need to do to finish your monster is add a large set of stitches across the forehead and another set down the side of one of the cheeks (Figure 83). The stitches can be made to look gruesome by adding a small amount of black or purple with a little red for blood. (See page 84 for a detailed description for making cuts and stitches.)

Figure 82

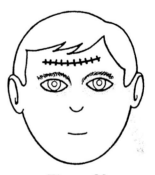

Figure 83

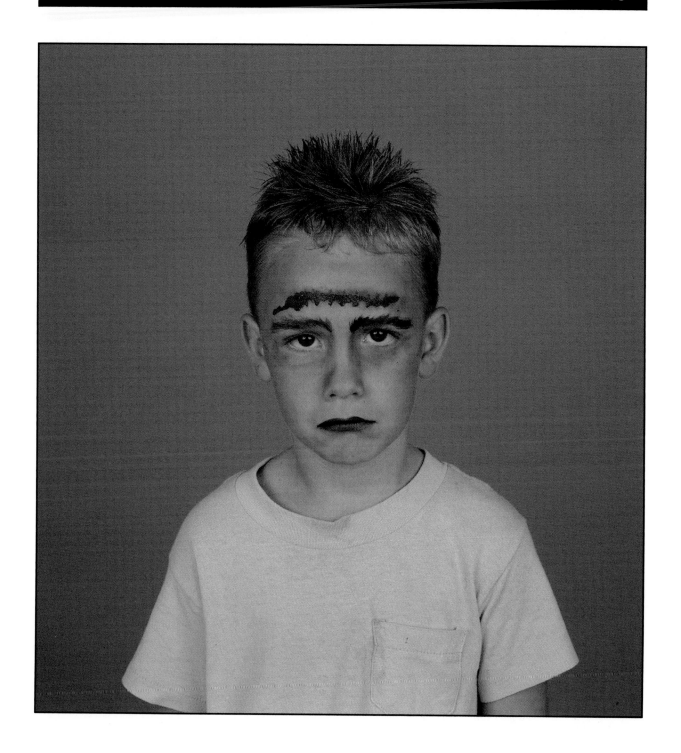

Werewolf

The Werewolf is the same as the basic tiger design, but using only black and brown. The muzzle is a little more pronounced and the nose is slightly larger. What really makes the werewolf different from the tiger are the thinner lines around the face made to resemble facial hair.

Make the tiger design as described on page 22.

Draw in the facial hair starting at the center of the forehead. Go around the face filling it with short, close strokes. Repeat the procedure in a second color (Figure 84).

Add fangs at the corner of the mouth. For a dramatic effect, put a little blood at the end of each fang (Figure 85).

Figure 84

Figure 85

Witch

Apply a thin layer of green to the entire face using a moist sponge. As in the Dracula design, make gray by mixing a little black and white and use it to shade the nose, eye area, and also the cheeks.

Darken the eyebrows with several small strokes to resemble hair (Figure 86).

Add one or two birthmarks or moles somewhere on the face. Color the lips in purple, red, or black (Figure 87).

If you want to make a more sinister looking witch, you can use black paint to make cat-like eye designs like the Tiger or the Werewolf, then shade the skin between the eyelids and eyebrows (Figure 88).

Figure 86

Figure 87

Figure 88

Skull

This face is very dramatic and best for older kids.

Cover the entire face with white makeup. Instead of using plain white paint, you could create a grayish, monster-like shade by mixing the white with a little bit of black or brown.

Draw two large circles around the eyes with black and carefully color them in (Figure 89). Draw a straight mouth as in Figure 90 and wait a few seconds for the paint to completely dry before continuing.

Using white, draw upper and lower teeth to create the skeleton look (Figure 91). A few crooked lines will give the design a really dramatic look (Figure 92). For the best effects when taking pictures, have the skull's eyes closed!

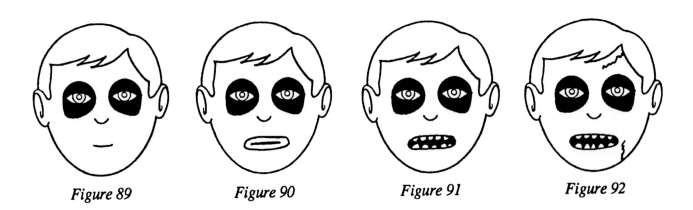

Figure 89   *Figure 90*   *Figure 91*   *Figure 92*

Dead Body

Older kids love the dead body because it's gross and the bullet hole, if done properly, looks very real! I'm not much into violence, but this design is very much in demand during Halloween and, if you learn to do it right, can be a lot of fun for the kids (and adults) who wear it. I do a lot of monsters for adults who want to party. It's only pretend, so have fun with it!

With a sponge, apply a light gray color (white mixed with a little black) to the entire face. Using a darker gray shade around the eyes (Figure 93).

To create the bullet hole effect, start by painting a series of small dots in black, purple, blue and red on the middle of the forehead. Then, using your finger, mix them together to create the appearance of a bruise-like wound (see pages 84-85 for a complete description of this process). Using black, draw a circle in the middle of the wound.

Add the blood to make it look as if it were dripping (Figure 94).

Paint the lips black. For a dramatic effect, add a little blood dripping from the mouth.

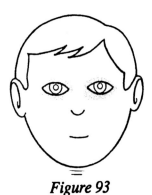

Figure 93

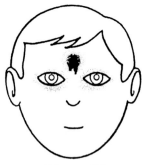

Figure 94

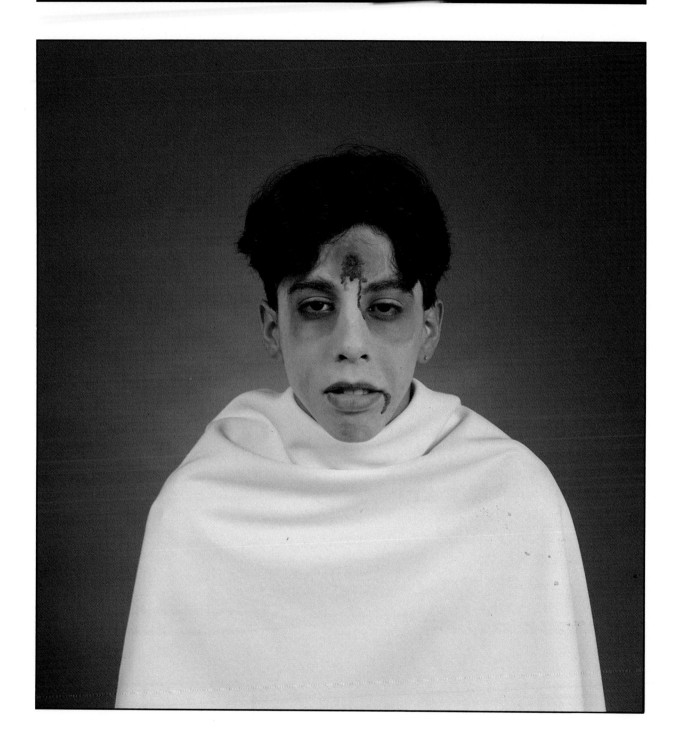

Cuts and Bruises

A quick and simple cut can be made by drawing a black line and putting a thin red line next to it. Stitches can be added if you desire (Figure 95).

An open cut can be drawn with two thin black lines paralleling each other and connected at the ends. Using fake blood or red paint, color the space between them. Adding stitches creates an ugly wound (Figure 96).

To create a bruise or black eye, paint several dots on the skin using black, red, purple, and blue (Figure 97). Mix the colors together with your finger or a sponge as shown in Figure 98. This is the same process you use for creating the wound in the Dead

Body, only the bullet hole is left out.

For a more dramatic effect, you can combine the bruise with the cut and the stitches (Figure 99). Add fake blood to the cut (Figure 100). The blood is what does it!

Experiment on your own and see what effects you can create. It's gross, but fun.

Now that you now how to create bullet holes, bruises, cuts, and stitches, and know how to make monster-like shading around the eyes, you can have fun creating you own monsters, ghosts, goblins, and other scary stuff.

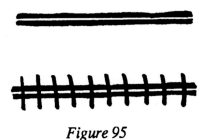

Figure 95

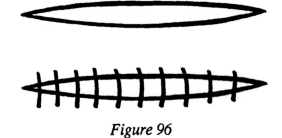

Figure 96

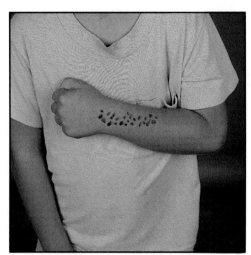

Figure 97

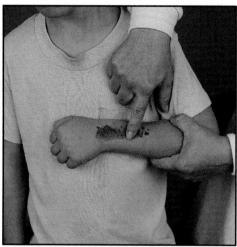

Figure 98

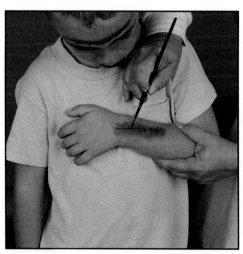

Figure 99

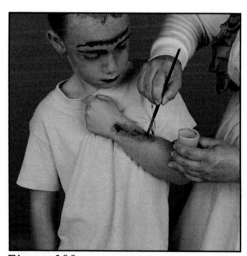

Figure 100

Tattoos

A tattoo is a simple drawing such as a small rainbow, flower, butterfly, or unicorn. Tattoos can be painted on the cheeks, the arms, and even the knees and feet. A single tattoo such as a rainbow or flower on the cheek serves as a quick and easy face painting design Some people use tattoos alone in their face painting.

If you are good with a small brush and with details, tattoos alone are a lot of fun and kids love them just as much. Once I painted happy faces on the big toes of some kids at a pajama party and they went around making their toes talk to each other.

Tattoos are good when you have a very long line or are short on time. They can be a day saver! Good examples are Batman and Ninja Turtle faces. Once you do one, all of the kids will want them.

For best results when painting tattoos, use colors that complement their hair color, eye color, complex- ion, or clothes. This will produce a design that matches the person being painted.

Some children, for whatever reason, do not like to have their faces painted. Assure them that you will never do anything they don't want you to do. Encourage them to have something painted on their hands. By seeing something small on their hands first, they will usually lose their fear of having their faces painted.

Some children may be afraid that the paint will not come off. By drawing a small design on your own hand, then removing it with a baby wipe, you can show them how easily it comes off and that there's absolutely nothing to worry about. When they realize that there's nothing to fear, the majority of them will let you paint their faces.

A tattoo can be just about anything you can draw.

The simplest are shapes such as hearts, stars, or rainbows. Except for snakes, animals are a little bit more difficult and so are characters like Mickey Mouse and the Ninja Turtles. Cartoon characters are very popular.

In the next few pages, I've prepared several designs for you to study and practice. Use various colors and experiment with the designs. Good luck!

APPENDIX

SOURCES OF MATERIALS

Theater, costume, magic and novelty shops carry quality makeup supplies. Many good toy stores also have paints and supplies suitable for face painting. When buying paint, look for water-soluble makeup. If your area does not have a makeup supplier with the proper materials, you can receive a catalog from a number of manufacturers and cosmetic dealers. Good quality makeup supplies suitable for face painting can be obtained from the following sources. Some of the manufacturers listed here do not sell directly to the public, but they will have a list of merchants who do carry their makeup supplies.

Ben Nye Company, Inc.
5935 Bowcroft Street
Los Angeles, CA 90016

Bob Kelly Cosmetics, Inc.
151 West 46th Street
New York, NY 10036

Kryolan Corporation
132 Ninth Street
San Francisco, CA 94103

Marcela "Mama Clown" Murad
230 South 14th Avenue
Hollywood, FL 33020

Mehron, Inc.
45 East Route 303
Valley Cottage, NY 10989

M. Stein Cosmetic Co.
10 Henery Stree
reeport, NY 11520

BIBLIOGRAPHY

Listed below are a few good books that can help further your knowledge on face painting and makeup techniques.

Alegre, Jean-Paul. *Party Make-up* Paradis-Circus, 1978

Boucher, Helene. *Make-up Magic* Les Editions Heritage Inc., 1989

Buchman, Herman. *Stage Makeup.* Watson-Guptill Publications, 1971

Fife, Bruce, et al. *Creative Clowning,* Piccadilly Books, 1988

Haldane, Suzanne. *Painting Faces,* E.P. Dutton, 1988

Jans, Martin. *Stage Makeup Techniques,* Players Press, Inc., 1986

Roberts, Jim. *Strutter's Complete Guide to Clown Makeup,* Piccadilly Books, 1991